LOVING THE EARTH

Also by Fredric Lehrman

THE SACRED LANDSCAPE

LOVING THE EARTH

A **Sacred Landscape** Book for Children

Written by FREDRIC LEHRMAN

Illustrated by LISA TUNE

CELESTIALARTS

Berkeley, California

CELESTIAL ARTS
P.O. Box 7327
Berkeley, CA 94707

Jacket and text design by David Charlsen
Typography by Recorder Typesetting Network
Photos supplied by Allstock/Seattle, WA and Wernher Krutein
    Photo Vault/San Francisco, CA

ISBN 0-89087-603-7
Library of Congress Catalog Card Number: 90-81947

First Printing, 1990

0 9 8 7 6 5 4 3 2 1
94 93 92 91 90

Manufactured in Hong Kong

This book is a project of Nomad University, a non-profit educational foundation which sponsors an international network of outstanding teachers and programs for self-directed students of all ages.

For further information, write to Nomad University, P.O. Box 2128, Seattle, WA 98111.

To William Ricketts,
who has kept the love of the Earth
young in his heart
for ninety years;
to Paul and Pamela and Olivia,
who are just beginning;
and to all of us,
Earth's children.

The earth is where we live. It is a big ball like the moon. If we went to the moon and looked up we would see the earth turning among the stars.

The moon is white. There are no plants there, and no water. There is no air and no sound. The sky is black. There is no wind. It is very different from here on the earth where we are.

SPACE is what is in between the earth and the moon. Space has no air in it. That is why it has no color; there is nothing in it to catch the light.

But the earth does have air around it, and that
makes all the difference.

Here on the earth there are many colors. The sky is blue. The leaves are green. The flowers and the birds and the fish and the animals and the insects are all different colors.

Here on earth the sky does many things. It makes all kinds of clouds. Some are long and flat; others are round and fluffy. The wind blows the clouds around in the sky.

Every time we breathe, we are taking the sky inside our bodies. It gives us energy. That's why we breathe all the time.

Take a big breath. See how your chest fills up? That's the sky inside you. Now relax and let the air go out again. When you breathe you are letting a little bit of the sky come in for a visit.

The sun offers the earth all its light. It makes the earth warm. It makes the sky glow. It is like a big campfire in the sky. If we face the fire we get warm; if we turn away we get cold.

The earth twirls around in front of the sun's fire. The earth is so big that it takes a whole day just for it to spin around once. That's why we have daytime and nighttime—daytime when we look towards the sun, nighttime when we are spinning around to look at it again.

17

The sun is really *very* big, but it is so far away that it looks small. The earth likes the sun, and goes around and around it all the time. Every time you have your birthday it means the earth has gone all the way around the sun one more time. And so have you, by the way!

All the different plants grow toward the sun. The big trees grow very high, but even the littlest plant knows where the sun is.

Plants drink water through their roots, which grow down into the earth. They breathe in air through their leaves, and send it back out all fresh and clean.

Each plant has its own special work and special reason for being here. Plants help us in lots of different ways. They give us food to eat, and fiber to weave with, and wood to build with. Some plants are useful for healing. And the pretty flowers remind us to be beautiful and to smell sweet. Always remember to thank the plants for what they give us.

Water washes everything and helps everything grow. Rivers and streams are roads that water makes to get to the sea. Water falls from the sky, carries things to the sea, and goes back up to the sky again.

Have you noticed that it's always cloudy before it rains? The clouds are water waiting to come down again.

We take water from streams, rivers, ponds, and lakes, and from deep wells in the ground. We drink it to keep our bodies cool and soft. We wash with it to make ourselves fresh and clean. Water is good for so many things!

The mountains are places where the earth reaches up into the sky. They are like very big people who can see far because they are so tall. The mountains are old and mighty and wise.

People go up on the mountains to breathe the clean air and to look at the stars and to hear the earth and the sky talking to each other.

The earth has lots of different kinds of places. There are high, high mountains and deep, deep valleys.

The deserts are empty and dry.

The jungles are moist and filled with plants.

The prairies are flat and covered with grass.

The top and bottom of the earth are cold and wear caps made of ice.

Every kind of place has its own
special plants and animals and birds
and insects and fish. And the people
in each place like to wear different
kinds of clothes, eat different kinds
of food, sing different kinds of
songs, dance different kinds of
dances, and play different kinds of
games. This is because of the way it
feels to live there.

The way a place feels is very important, because how it feels outside is part of how you feel inside.

How does it feel where *you* live?

Do you have a favorite place in your house where you like to sit? You can find places like this outside too. Maybe there is a special rock you can lean against, or a special tree which you can sit under, or a special hill you can stand on top of. Each place has its own kind of feeling.

In some places the feeling is so good that lots of people like to go there.

Always look for the magic spots wherever you go. You'll find that if you are quiet and pay attention, and wait, you can learn all kinds of things from these places. You might even hear the Earth talking to you.

This next part is very important.
Because the Earth is a big ball, and
the sky and the ocean are wrapped
around it, the air and water from one
place can easily float to another place
on the other side of the Earth. There
is nothing to stop it from flowing
there. What people throw away on
the other side of the Earth ends up
here, and what we throw away ends
up there. So we have to think about
keeping the water and the air as
clean as we can.

Whatever grows from the Earth can
be put back on the Earth without
causing any trouble. The Earth
makes apples, so it's alright if an
apple falls off a tree onto the ground.
It will eventually become part of the
Earth again. But there are lots of
things which people have made
which the Earth can't use. The Earth
can't use plastic so we should never
throw anything made of plastic onto
the Earth and leave it there, because
it will just sit there forever and get in
the way.

There are other things which the Earth can't use, but *we* can use them over again. Empty bottles and cans and old cloth and paper are things that can be collected instead of being thrown away. These things can be made into useful new things. Then the Earth won't have to keep giving us new metal and wood and sand for things which we use just one time and throw away.

We all need to start being nice to the Earth, to be *its friend*. That's what this book is about. Everyone can learn to work together to make the Earth happy.

Wouldn't it be nice if everything we built fit in with the land and the sky and made the Earth feel better? We are learning how to do this. First we need to keep things clean. We need to plant more trees and flowers everywhere. We need to make our homes feel the way we like the Earth to feel.

As you grow up, you can learn more and more ways to make the Earth happy. If we listen to what the Earth wants, and help the plants and the animals and the water and the sky, then they will all help us, and everything will start to feel better and better and better.

Some people are so busy that they have forgotten all about this. You can help them remember by telling them what you know and asking them to love the Earth too. Ask them to go for a walk with you and tell you about the air and the water and the land. Ask them to help you plant a tree. Ask them to help you clean up a place that has gotten dirty.

Remember that the Earth has given us all our food and everything we need to live. Now we have to start giving gifts back to the Earth. If we want to get good things, we have to give good things. It is time to start loving the Earth. It is time to start thanking the Earth for letting us be here.

So now you know. Why don't you go outside today, and look at the sky, or a rock, or a tree, or a stream, or a lake, or a hill, or a field, or the ocean, and thank it for being there. Then ask it what it would like from you. If you listen long enough, it will tell you what you can do to make it happy. Then soon you will be able to say:

The Earth is my best friend!

SOME QUESTIONS AND ANSWERS ABOUT WHY THE EARTH IS THE WAY IT IS

This next part is for those of you who wonder about how things work. The Earth is a very interesting place and there are a lot of things to learn about it.

Remember, the Earth is a very big ball. You can start in any direction and go all the way around. The top of the ball is called North. The bottom of the ball is called South. The Earth spins like a top. The direction it spins in is called East. The direction it leaves behind is called West.

The spinning Earth moves around the sun in a big loop. A big ball which flies through space and goes around a sun is called a PLANET. So this is PLANET EARTH.

You might be wondering, "If the Earth is a ball, why does it look flat; and if it is spinning through space, why don't I feel it moving? Why does it feel like it is just standing still?"

These are good questions. Here are some good answers.

The Earth looks flat because it is so big. If you sail away in a boat, the ocean looks flat. But after awhile you might look back and you won't be able to see the place where you got on the boat. This is because you have gone far enough around the curve of the Earth so that the place you left behind is out of sight. We say that it is "below the horizon," which is the line where the sky meets the Earth.

But if you go high enough in a *space*ship, you can look down and see the roundness of the Earth very easily. *(See photo on p. 7)*

Something to do: *Kneel down on the floor. Put your cheek flat on the floor and look around. How much of the floor can you see? Now lift you head up slowly and see how everything changes. The higher you are, the farther you can see!*

Why don't we feel the Earth moving? It's because we are moving *with* it. Do you know how sometimes you can be riding in a car, and if you close your eyes, it feels almost like you're standing still? Well, the Earth is like a very big car, and we've been riding on it ever since we were born. We've never felt it speed up or slow down. It always goes the same speed, and we go right along with it. That's why we think it is standing still.

Something to do: *Go out into a field or an open space with a friend. Hold hands with each other and run. Try running so well together that you feel like one person. This is how it feels to move with the Earth.*

Now comes a really big question. If the Earth is a ball spinning through space, why doesn't everything start falling off? Why doesn't the water in the ocean just fly away?

Nobody *really* knows the answer to this question, but we know that the Earth wants to keep everything that comes near it. It is like a magnet for everything. We call this pull of the Earth GRAVITY. When we are on the Earth, things feel heavy. This is because of gravity.

Gravity is a very good thing. It never forgets its job. It keeps things where you put them. Imagine what it would be like if everything in your room started floating around. It would be hard to keep things straight, and some things might float out the window and get lost. So remember to thank the Earth for helping you by keeping the gravity turned on.

If you want to know what it would feel like to be without gravity, there are three good ways. The first is to become an astronaut. Then you can travel way out into space to where the Earth lets go. Then everything starts floating.

The second way is by swimming under water. Then you can float like the fish.

The third way is when you are asleep. In your dreams you can fly and float and do anything you want.

There are many things you can do to understand more about the Earth. Here are some ideas to start with.

Something to do: *Put a lamp in the middle of the room. Then turn out all the other lights. Stand a little bit away from the lamp. Then turn around slowly, all the way around. You are the earth and the light bulb is the sun. If you moved so slowly that it took you a whole day just to turn around once, you would see the light move past you just the way you see the sun moving across the sky every day.*

Something to do: *With your lamp in the middle of the room, and the other lights out, walk all the way around the room once, making the circle as big as you can. Now do it again, only this time spin as you go around. If you went so slowly that you took a whole year to go around the room once, and you spun around only once each day, you'd be moving around the lamp just the way the earth moves around the sun.*

Something to do: *Go around your house and find everything that was made from a plant—food, cotton, linen, wood, perfume, herbs and medicines, paper— and thank the plants for helping you.*

Something to do: *Look on a globe or a map of the Earth and find out where you are. Put your finger on that spot and then ask these questions:*

What does it look like in this place?
What kinds of plants live here?
What kinds of animals and birds and fish and insects live here?
Is it hot or cold here?
Is it rainy or sunny?
What do the people here like to wear?
What kinds of food do they eat?
What kinds of songs do they sing?

When you have learned the answers to these questions, put your finger on another spot on the globe. Ask the questions again and learn all the things you can about what it is like in the new place.

Pretty soon you'll know about how things are all over the Earth.

Here is a list of a few words which we need to know in order to be able to talk about caring for the Earth.

ACID RAIN—rain which comes down with smoke from factories in it and makes trees and plants and fish feel bad and get sick.

ATMOSPHERE—the air which wraps around the Earth. We breathe the air from the atmosphere.

BIODEGRADABLE—if the Earth can use something again after we are finished with it we say it is biodegradable, which means that it is easy for nature to take it apart and make something new and good with it.

BIOLOGY—the study of how living things work.

BIOSPHERE—all the living things across the surface of the Earth—people, animals, birds, insects, fish, plants, and the air and water and light which feed them.

BOTANY—the study of plants and flowers.

CLIMATE—the way the weather is in a particular place—how hot or cold it is, and how much rain falls there.

DEFORESTATION—cutting too many trees too fast so that the forest can't catch up and starts to die.

ECOLOGY—the study of how to help each thing in nature work well with every other thing.

ECOSYSTEM—the way in which all the plants and animals and the climate and the water in a particular place work together.

ENERGY—the power of the universe which we use to make things work. Most things get their energy originally from the sun.

THE ENVIRONMENT—the physical world we live in.

FORESTRY—the science of taking care of forests.

GREENHOUSE EFFECT—the atmosphere is starting to heat up like a greenhouse because we have made the air dirty. This keeps the hotness of the sunlight from getting back out into space where it came from so that the Earth can cool off again.

OIL SPILLS—oil or gasoline which leaks from boats into the ocean and makes life hard for fish, animals and birds. The oil floats around until it gets stuck on something like a beach or your feet. It is sticky and smelly.

POLLUTION—what happens when we spoil the air or the water or the land by putting unhealthy things into them.

RAINFORESTS—the biggest and most important forests—the plants and trees in the rainforests are the best workers to keep the air clean and remove pollution from the atmosphere.

RECYCLING—when we take something that we've already used once, and clean it up and use it again instead of just throwing it away. This makes everything last longer, and we don't need to keep taking new materials from the Earth all the time.

RENEWABLE ENERGY—when we make things work by using power from things which don't run out, like sunlight, wind, flowing water, or heat from inside the Earth.

SPHERE—something that is round like a ball. Planet Earth is a sphere.

There are many other words which you will learn as you talk about these things with your friends, your parents, and your teachers. Maybe some of you will even someday want to become ecologists or biologists or botanists. But every one of us can be environmentalists right now just by caring more about how we treat the Earth, and starting to do things together to help the Earth to breathe, to flow, and to grow.

It's important, and no one is too young to start working for Planet Earth.

Thank you for reading this book.

Photo Credits

Front cover–Tom Bean

Back cover–Chris Arend

Page 1–Jim Brandenburg

Page 7–Courtesy of NASA

Page 21–Pat O'Hara

Page 28–Art Wolfe (*top*)
      Donald Graham (*bottom*)

Page 29–Will/Deni McIntyre (*top*)
      Tim Thompson (*middle*)
      Art Wolfe (*bottom*)

Pages 30 & 31–Christopher Arnesen, Jim Corwin, Bruce Forster, Rick Furniss, Wernher
      Krutein, Will McIntyre, Don & Pat Valenti

Page 33–Ross Hamilton

Page 34–Phil Schermeister (*top*)
      Pat O'Hara (*bottom*)

Page 35–Hooke

Page 36–Pat O'Hara (*left*)
      David Muench (*right*)

Page 37–James Stuart (*left*)
      Tom Bean (*right*)

Page 38–M. Thonig

Page 41–Bill Ross

Page 47–Stephen Hilson